REBEL GIRLS CLIMATE WARRIORS

25 TALES OF WOMEN WHO PROTECT THE EARTH

Good Night Stories for Rebel Girls and Rebel Girls are registered trademarks. *Good Night Stories for Rebel Girls* and all other Rebel Girls titles are available for bulk purchase for sale promotions, premiums, fundraising, and educational needs. For details, write to sales@rebelgirls.com.

This is a work of creative nonfiction. It is a collection of heartwarming and thought-provoking stories inspired by the lives and adventures of 26 influential women and girls. It is not an encyclopedic account of the events and accomplishments of their lives.

www.rebelgirls.com

Some of the artwork in this book has been previously published in the books *Good Night Stories for Rebel Girls, Good Night Stories for Rebel Girls 2, Good Night Stories for Rebel Girls: 100 Immigrant Women Who Changed the World*, and *Good Night Stories for Rebel Girls: 100 Real-Life Tales of Black Girl Magic*.

Text by Abby Sher, Nana Brew-Hammond, Sam Guss, Sarah Parvis, and Susanna Daniel
Art direction by Giulia Flamini
Cover illustrations by Annalisa Ventura
Graphic design by Annalisa Ventura and Kristen Brittain
Special thanks: Emilee Jayne Moore, Grace House, Kait Bergun, Maithy Vu, Marina Asenjo

Printed in Italy, 2021
10 9 8 7 6 5 4 3 2 1
ISBN: 978-1-953424-21-1

FSC
www.fsc.org
MIX
Paper from
responsible sources
FSC® C013123

CONTENTS

Dear Rebels,

Growing up in Morelos, Mexico, just south of Mexico City, I couldn't always get to the sea. But I was fascinated by it. I loved to flip through my brother's copy of a book by legendary explorer and photographer Jacques Cousteau. The undersea pictures were amazing! I wanted to dive into them and glide through the water with a pod of dolphins. I wanted to see towering forests of kelp or enormous blue whales with my own eyes. I didn't have words for it at the time, but I felt it deeply: those photos had power!

I got a degree in marine science, and for my first adult job, I cataloged wildlife in a beach town called Akumal. At night, I watched sea turtles scoot out of the sea and lay their eggs in shallow little nests on the beach. But in the morning, seagulls and raccoons would come along and eat the eggs! I was incredibly sad for the sea turtles. They are so important for our ecosystem. So I did what I could. I moved the eggs at night to keep them safe.

Years later, I became a photographer for *National Geographic* magazine and then struck out on my own, eventually forming the International League of Conservation Photographers, SeaLegacy, and Only One. For many years now, I've used my camera to tell stories about the oceans and the animals and plants that live underwater. If I can capture people's attention, then they can learn that the oceans hold the secrets to healing the planet.

I know images can help persuade people about the urgent need to protect wild places. That's why Paul Nicklen and I founded SeaLegacy, an organization that brings together the world's top photographers, filmmakers, conservationists, and scientists to use visual storytelling to excite and engage people in ocean conservation. Today, I am the cofounder and president of SeaLegacy and Only One.

But you don't need to be a scientist or the president of an organization to help. You can use your talents as a writer, singer, or storyteller to spread the word and join the fight against human-made pollution and climate change.

The Rebel Girls in this book are doing just that—and in wildly different ways. Julia Butterfly Hill lived in a giant redwood tree for more than two years to keep loggers from cutting it down. Nemonte Nenquimo sued the Ecuadorian government to protect land that belonged to the Waorani people from being auctioned off for oil exploration. And Angelina Arora made a plastic alternative using shrimp shells!

Saving the planet is an enormous task, but no single person has to tackle it alone or all at once. When you see something that needs to change, do what you can to change it. In Southampton, England, Ella and Caitlin McEwan were upset that the plastic toys given out by fast food restaurants ended up in landfills or washed out to sea. So they started a petition that convinced companies to change their policies. For Esohe Ozigbo, it was the trash piling up in the streets and clogging up streams in her neighborhood in Lagos, Nigeria, that spurred her to action.

No matter where you live or what your interests are, there is something you can do to help make the world a greener, healthier place for us all.

So whether you are 9 years old or 90, whether you live by the sea or have never touched it, know that you can make a difference. Do not lose hope. Even though an action may feel small at first, remember that small actions can add up to meaningful change.

We need an army of dreamers, doers, and storytellers. We need Rebels.

Please join us.

—Cristina Mittermeier, SeaLegacy/Only One

SCAN TO HEAR MORE!

BONUS! AUDIO STORIES!

Download the Rebel Girls app to hear longer stories about some of the dedicated planet protectors in this book. You will also unlock creative activities and discover stories of other trailblazing women. Whenever you come across a bookmark icon, scan the code, and you'll be whisked away on an audio adventure.

ANGELINA ARORA

INVENTOR

One day, Angelina was at the supermarket when the cashier asked her to pay for a plastic bag. The cashier explained that plastic takes hundreds of years to decompose in landfills, and that plastic bags often end up in the ocean. So Australia had passed laws to help reduce plastic waste.

When it came time to do her ninth grade science project, Angelina thought about what the cashier had said. *What if I could develop a more natural plastic—a bioplastic—that didn't harm the Earth?* she thought.

Angelina experimented with cornstarch, potato starch, and even old banana peels. Nothing worked. Then she went out for fish and chips and had a wild idea. Looking down at a pile of shrimp shells tossed in the trash, she noticed something. The shiny, almost see-through shells looked a lot like plastic. *What are they made of?* she wondered.

She soon learned that shrimp shells contain a material called chitin. Some scientists were already using chitin to make bioplastics because it's sturdy and doesn't dissolve in water. Plus, there's a lot of it! Australia produces 75,000 tons of seafood waste every year. With so much material at hand, it seemed silly *not* to make plastic out of shrimp!

After a lot of trial and error, Angelina cooked up a recipe that combined chitin and a chemical found in silkworm cocoons. Her bioplastic is unusually good. It's strong, flexible, and foldable. While most plastic takes 400 years to break down, Angelina's takes just 33 days. And it doesn't release harmful chemicals into the environment. When Angelina's plastic breaks down in dirt, it gives off a chemical that actually helps plants grow!

BIRTHDATE UNKNOWN

AUSTRALIA

"PLEASE JOIN ME
IN MY JOURNEY IN
PAVING THE WAY
TOWARD A GREENER
FUTURE. BELIEVE
ME, WE CAN DO IT."
—ANGELINA ARORA

ANNE HIDALGO

POLITICIAN

Before she was the mayor of Paris, Anne was a little Spanish girl in San Fernando, Spain. Born Ana María to a father who was an electrician and a mother who was a seamstress, Anne moved to Lyon, France, with her family when she was two years old.

But she had trouble fitting in. When she was in second grade, her teacher told her that little Spanish girls don't make it to the top of the class. Anne was ready to prove her wrong.

At 14 years old, Anne became a French citizen. Later, she began to study social services and law. She saw how hard it was for people to get housing or enjoy the outdoors. She wanted to work in government so she could help people and change the way cities were structured. Anne loved Paris and its ancient monuments and cathedrals. But what about its future? There were so many congested roads, polluted rivers, and parks covered in concrete. Anne was determined to make the city greener.

In 2014, Anne became the first-ever woman to be elected mayor of Paris. Since then, she has transformed the city. She banned cars from certain streets and helped build miles of new bike lanes to cut pollution. She had thousands of new trees planted and invested in green roofs, electric buses, and free public transportation. She also helped draft the Paris Agreement, which is a plan and promise from many nations to fight climate change.

"We've rediscovered quite simple things," Anne says about her work— simple but amazing, like the joy of smelling cherry blossoms in the spring or finding shade on a hot summer day.

BORN JUNE 19, 1959
SPAIN AND FRANCE

ILLUSTRATION BY
ALICE PIAGGIO

"MY VISION FOR
PARIS IS AS A GREEN
CITY WHERE WE CAN
ALL BREATHE FRESH
AIR, SHARE OPEN
SPACE, AND ENJOY
OUR LIVES."
—ANNE HIDALGO

AUTUMN PELTIER

CLEAN WATER ACTIVIST

Once upon a time, there was a girl who believed that all water was sacred. Her name was Autumn, and she was born in the Wikwemikong Unceded Indian Reserve, on Manitoulin Island, Canada.

Autumn loved being silly, making slime with her sister, and texting with friends. But she was very serious about protecting the water people drink and the water that nourishes animals and plants and allows trees to grow tall.

Growing up in the Ojibwe/Odawa heritage, Autumn began performing water ceremonies when she was very little. She would walk through fierce winter winds with her elders and kneel on a frozen lake. She'd make a hole in the ice and dip in a special copper cup, scooping out water and chanting a prayer of protection.

When Autumn was eight years old, she attended a water ceremony. Signs all over read, "DON'T DRINK THE WATER." She learned that underground pipelines had contaminated the water. It broke her heart.

In 2016, Autumn was chosen to present the Canadian prime minister with a special gift at an annual gathering for the First Nations. With thousands of eyes watching, she took a deep breath and handed him a copper water bowl. Then she said, "I am very unhappy with the choices you've made."

She told him that he was hurting her people by allowing pipelines to pollute their water. The crowd was shocked and inspired, and the prime minister promised to help.

Since that day, Autumn has traveled around the world, raising her voice and demanding that leaders respect and protect our waters. As she says, "Water is everything. It's the lifeblood of Mother Earth."

BORN SEPTEMBER 27, 2004

CANADA

ILLUSTRATION BY
JING LI

"WE ALL NEED
WATER. WE
WOULDN'T BE
ABLE TO LIVE
WITHOUT WATER.
NOTHING WOULD."
—AUTUMN PELTIER

BERNICE NOTENBOOM

CLIMATE JOURNALIST AND FILMMAKER

As a baby, Bernice was always climbing out of her playpen. She was an escape artist!

This adventurous little girl would grow up to be an explorer, writing about her journeys in *National Geographic* magazine. But when she was 45 years old, a trip to the North Pole changed her life completely.

Few people go to the North Pole. The conditions are brutal. In addition to the cold and wind, the ice is constantly moving underfoot. There is a threat of running into a hungry polar bear. And explorers have to haul all of their food and gear in sleds that they pull along the ice. There are a ton of reasons *not* to go to the Arctic. But Bernice went anyway.

As she trekked across the frozen landscape, she saw water where there should have been thick, glistening ice. The ice was so thin in so many places that Bernice's party couldn't reach their destination. They got stuck miles from the Pole without enough food. All around them, cracks in the ice were wide and deep. Waiting for rescue, Bernice realized that this was what climate change really looked like: a continent of ice crumbling into pieces. She decided that from then on she would travel to all of the places most affected by climate change and tell their stories.

She went to Siberia, back to the North Pole, to the South Pole, and to Greenland. She wrote books and helped make documentaries that showed how badly the Earth needed help. She gave lectures and took business executives to see the ice caps melting in real time.

Now Bernice travels not for the sake of adventure but to honor a higher calling: to save the world.

BORN JUNE 1, 1962

THE NETHERLANDS

ILLUSTRATION BY
GEORGIE STEWART

"WE HAVE NO TIME TO LOSE—
AND SEEING IS BELIEVING."
—BERNICE NOTENBOOM

DANNI WASHINGTON

OCEAN ADVOCATE

Once upon a time, there was a girl who longed to live under the sea and learn from schools of fish. Her name was Danni.

When she was near the ocean, you'd find her diving deep below the surface. When she was on land, she was either reading a book about the sea or splashing around in her grandparents' pool. She went to ocean camp and dreamed of being a mermaid. At 17, she became a certified scuba diver.

After studying marine biology in college, Danni was even more in awe of the power under the sea. She wanted everyone to know that underwater kelp keeps 20 times more carbon dioxide out of the atmosphere than land forests, and that the plankton that glitter like colored glass in the water also remove carbon from the air. If the ocean were free from human-made pollution, Danni believed, undersea life could save the planet from climate change.

At 21, she started a nonprofit organization called Big Blue & You with her mom to teach kids how to be ocean advocates. Later, she created the Mocha Mermaid community to connect scientists of color. Sometimes, she put on bright fishtails to help spread her message as a mermaid. Danni made it her mission to get on one of the biggest platforms on Earth: television. She snapped on goggles, stepped into flippers, strapped her oxygen tank to her back, and dove underwater on camera to share what she knew about sea life. She scored a spot on a science show that was broadcast to millions.

The ocean's the limit for Danni. She'll keep helping the next generation of ocean warriors understand that safeguarding Earth's waters—the source of at least half the oxygen people breathe—is critical to slowing the climate crisis. As always, she's ready to dive in.

BORN DECEMBER 30, 1986

UNITED STATES OF AMERICA

"IF IT WAS EASY TO SOLVE THE CLIMATE CRISIS, WE WOULD HAVE SOLVED IT ALREADY. WE'VE GOT A LOT OF WORK TO DO, AND WE NEED EVERYONE INVOLVED."
—DANNI WASHINGTON

ILLUSTRATION BY FANESHA FABRE

ELLA AND CAITLIN McEWAN

CLIMATE ACTIVISTS

One day, Ella and her sister Caitlin were eating fast food when they noticed something about the free toys that came with their meals: they were made entirely out of hard plastic. The sisters had learned about the dangers of plastic in school—how it took a very, very long time to break down naturally and how oceans were filling up with plastic trash. *Why were restaurants giving out so much of this stuff? Didn't they know these toys were often played with just once before getting tossed?*

The girls were outraged. *Someone has to stop this nonsense*, they decided, and began brainstorming what they could do to help. They started a petition, asking two popular companies to quit including hard plastic toys with their kids' meals in the United Kingdom. At first, the fast food giants ignored the McEwan sisters. They weren't scared of a seven and a nine-year-old in the English countryside. But as the petition gained attention from international media, the signature count began to climb: 100,000, then 200,000. Up, up, up it went. Half a million kids and their parents agreed with Ella and Caitlin.

Finally, one of the companies caved. It would stop giving out plastic toys in the UK, saving a whopping 350 tons of plastic a year from ending up in landfills or washing out to sea. The second company changed its tune too. It promised to give out only soft toys and sustainable treats in the UK and Ireland. This meant another 3,300 tons of plastic wouldn't be tumbling out of kids' meals and going straight into the trash.

Ella and Caitlin were in awe. Though they were still in elementary school, they had spoken up. With the help of 510,000 new friends, they'd made a real difference.

BIRTHDATES UNKNOWN
UNITED KINGDOM

"IT'S NOT ENOUGH TO MAKE RECYCLABLE PLASTIC TOYS—BIG, RICH COMPANIES SHOULDN'T BE MAKING TOYS OUT OF PLASTIC AT ALL."
—ELLA AND CAITLIN McEWAN

ILLUSTRATION BY ANINE BÖSENBERG

ESOHE OZIGBO

CLIMATE ACTIVIST

Esohe always loved going to the beach with her friends. But instead of splashing in the waves or finding a clear stretch of sand to lie on, she and her crew would mask up, put on gloves, and pick up the litter that dotted the sand and bobbed in the surf. When they weren't doing seaside cleanups, they were removing trash and plastic waste from roadsides, fields, and parking lots. They trudged through mud and muck and streams to keep garbage from choking waterways in Lagos, Nigeria.

But their job was never done. There was always more litter to clear.

Esohe didn't want her city to become a dump. She wanted fish to swim in clean, healthy water. But how could she spread the word to the 20 million residents of her city? How could she let kids everywhere—and adults too!—know that tossing garbage on the ground can make animals sick, cause flooding, and spread disease?

Together with her friends, she collected and cleaned plastic bags, cups, bottle caps, and straws. Then she fashioned her finds into one-shoulder crop tops, swing skirts, colorful dresses, hoop earrings, necklaces, and more.

Esohe turned trash into "trashion."

She teamed up with some local shopping malls to host runway trashion shows. Before she knew it, Esohe's outfits—made with everyday junk—gained the attention of fans far outside of Lagos. Reporters from all over came to check out the collection. They broadcast Esohe's work—and her message—to the world.

"We are the generation who are going to be leading in a few years," she says, "so we need to start now."

BORN CIRCA 2006

NIGERIA

ILLUSTRATION BY
RONIQUE ELLIS

"WE ARE JUST
TEENAGERS,
BUT WE ARE
TRYING TO MAKE
A CHANGE IN
THE WORLD."
—ESOHE OZIGBO

GRETA THUNBERG

CLIMATE ACTIVIST

Greta didn't think like most kids. She'd been diagnosed with Asperger's syndrome and obsessive-compulsive disorder (OCD). These conditions sometimes made her feel lonely, but they also allowed her to see the world in her own way.

At school, Greta's eyes grew wide as she watched a documentary about pollution in the oceans. Her heart sank as she learned that a massive pile of plastic the size of Mexico was floating in the Pacific Ocean. When the movie ended, other students went on with their day, but what Greta saw changed her life.

She saw something her classmates didn't see: an urgent crisis.

First, Greta reduced her own carbon footprint. She stopped riding in planes and cars, saved energy by turning off electrical outlets in her home, and stopped eating meat or dairy products.

But small changes weren't enough. After all, Greta was just one person. How could she stop heat waves, storms, and wildfires alone? Instead of giving up because the problem was too big, Greta marched to the Swedish parliament. She refused to go back to school until her country vowed to reduce its carbon emissions.

She began protesting every Friday and sharing her thoughts on social media. Inspired by Greta, thousands of students from more than 100 countries walked out of school too. They sent their message around the globe: the world is in trouble, and officials need to do something about it before it's too late. Fearlessly, Greta spoke directly to leaders worldwide. "The eyes of all future generations are upon you," she said.

BORN JANUARY 3, 2003
SWEDEN

"I DON'T WANT YOUR HOPE. I DON'T WANT YOU TO BE HOPEFUL. I WANT YOU TO PANIC."
—GRETA THUNBERG

HU WEIWEI

ENTREPRENEUR

Weiwei looked into the sky and frowned. Smoke-colored clouds hung over her city, and she was sick of it! The blackened sky wasn't announcing a storm—it was signaling dirt and chemicals. The air was polluted.

She remembered a time when the air in Beijing was clearer and her city was simpler—a time when most people rode bicycles because they didn't have cars. Fewer cars on the road meant less smoke sneezing out of exhaust pipes. Weiwei made it her mission to bring back bicycles.

But getting a city full of people pedaling to work and school—instead of sitting in heated or air-conditioned vehicles—was going to be tough. So Weiwei focused on making it as easy as possible to find a ride.

She created a bike-sharing company and called it Mobike.

Weiwei led her team to develop a lock that riders could open anywhere, anytime with their mobile phones. She had the bikes built with airless tires so riders would never get a flat. And she worked with the government to create bike lanes and parking spaces near major train and bus stops.

Still, it took a while to get people pedaling.

After a year in business, only 1,275 riders in Shanghai hopped on a Mobike, even though the city had more than 26 million people. Weiwei kept tinkering, released a new model, and oh did that one take off! Soon people were taking 20 million trips a day using Weiwei's great green idea.

By the end of 2017, 200 million riders were steering Mobikes all over 200 cities around the globe. Weiwei looks forward to a future when the air will be clear again—not just in her city but all around the world.

BORN 1982

CHINA

"THE HUMBLE BICYCLE CAN
NOT ONLY CHANGE PEOPLE
AND CITIES BUT CAN ALSO HELP
CHANGE THE WORLD—BOTH AS
A UNIVERSAL SYMBOL OF PEACE
AND AS A WEAPON IN THE FIGHT
AGAINST CLIMATE CHANGE."
—HU WEIWEI

ISATOU CEESAY

ACTIVIST AND SOCIAL ENTREPRENEUR

Isatou was born in 1972 in The Gambia, one of Africa's smallest countries. She grew up surrounded by peanut farms, wide blue skies, and mountains and mountains of trash. Her village was very poor, and there were no garbage trucks to come and collect the things people threw away. Animals were dying because they swallowed plastic bags. Mosquitoes buzzed around the water that collected in the junk and spread malaria. And when people burned plastic to make fires, terrible fumes filled the air.

Something needs to change, Isatou thought. In 1997, she opened the first recycling center in her village. She gathered five of her friends to collect and clean plastic bags. They cut the bags into long strips and used the "plarn" (plastic yarn) to crochet a purse. Their first purse took eight hours to make! But Isatou was thrilled. She had turned garbage into something beautiful and useful.

People told her she was dirty, digging around in other people's trash. Some men were alarmed because they thought women shouldn't work outside of the home. "I want to prove them wrong," said Isatou.

Within a year, she had 50 women working with her. They sold their bags, bracelets, and crafts at the market and earned money to support their families. Pretty soon, Isatou's village was out of plastic bags, so the women collected garbage from other villages and sold their creations all over the world. They made paper beads, truck tire armchairs, and more. And in 2015, The Gambia's government banned plastic bags!

Isatou's bright idea transformed trash into treasure, helped her community, and trained women to be the leaders of a cleaner future.

BORN DECEMBER 30, 1972
THE GAMBIA

ILLUSTRATION BY
NAKI NARH

"I THINK THAT WHEN
YOU ABUSE YOUR
ENVIRONMENT, YOU
ABUSE YOURSELF."
—ISATOU CEESAY

JAMIE MARGOLIN

CLIMATE ACTIVIST

Once there was a girl who felt anxious about everything. What if all the animals became extinct? What if the glaciers melted? What if all the coral reefs died? What if the city she grew up in was underwater by the time she was old enough to have kids of her own?

Jamie knew that all these terrible things could happen one day if people didn't come together to fight climate change. People had been polluting the environment for centuries, but kids like Jamie had had nothing to do with building factories, driving cars, and manufacturing plastics. Jamie felt like her generation would pay the price for the actions of people who came before.

Jamie knew that the best way to start a movement was to get her friends involved. So she reached out to a group of young activists she had connected with at a summer program. Even though they all lived in different areas of the country, Jamie and her friends spent hours together online each week, working out the details of their movement. Together they began to plan what would become Zero Hour.

After a year of meetings, Jamie and more than 100 of her Zero Hour peers headed to Washington, DC, to give lawmakers a list of demands: stop giving money to the fossil fuel industry, and stop accepting money from businesses that are destroying the planet. Zero Hour then led a youth march on the US Capitol. Thousands of young people in 25 countries around the world led sister marches in their own cities. They walked, with their signs raised high in the air, and chanted their heartfelt messages.

It turns out that a lot of kids were as anxious as Jamie was about climate change—and together, their voices were so loud the world had to listen.

BORN DECEMBER 10, 2001

UNITED STATES OF AMERICA

ILLUSTRATION BY
PAU ZAMRO

ZERO
HOUR

"I AM ESPECIALLY
PROUD OF BUILDIN
A MOVEMENT THAT IS
RUN BY WOMEN OF
COLOR. IT PROVI
A SAFE PLACE FO
GIRLS LIKE ME
—JAMIE MARGOLIN

JULIA BUTTERFLY HILL

ACTIVIST AND AUTHOR

The first time Butterfly saw the California redwoods, she dropped to her knees and cried. She had never seen anything so magical. But the beautiful, ancient trees in this forest were in danger. A lumber company was planning to chop them down for wood.

Butterfly joined a group of activists that were camped out in the forest. These people were tree-sitters. They took turns sitting high up in a redwood, guarding it night and day. No one would cut down a tree if a person was living in it.

This group of tree-sitters needed help. They needed someone to protect a tree by living in it for at least five days. But who on Earth would be willing to live on a tiny platform way up high in the sky for that long? Butterfly raised her hand. She was the only volunteer.

In 1997, Butterfly climbed up into the branches of a tree named Luna. She was 23 years old. Luna was much, much older.

After her five days were up, Butterfly decided to stay. With sap stuck to her feet, she moved through the branches of her beloved tree. When it was cold, she snuggled in a sleeping bag. She used a rope to pull up her food, medicine, and supplies. And 180 feet below Butterfly's perch, the world watched.

Finally, the lumber company agreed to let Luna stand. They also agreed not to touch the three acres of redwoods surrounding Luna! After more than two years, Butterfly climbed back down to rejoin the world below. She was celebrated as a hero. When she took her first steps on the ground, her legs were shaky—but she stood tall and proud. No one had ever sat up in a tree for as long as she had lived among Luna's branches and leaves.

BORN FEBRUARY 18, 1974
UNITED STATES OF AMERICA

"ANYONE WHO WANTS TO CUT A TREE LIKE THIS SHOULD SPEND TWO YEARS IN IT FIRST."
—JULIA BUTTERFLY HILL

KOTCHAKORN VORAAKHOM

LANDSCAPE ARCHITECT

Once upon a time, there was a girl called Kotchakorn who loved watching plants push through cracks in the concrete parking lot near her house. She would tug at the concrete, digging bigger holes so her little green friends had more room to grow. She had no idea those sneaky little weeds held the secret to her future—and her city's.

Kotchakorn lived in Bangkok, Thailand—a city that is slowly sinking under the river it was built on. Every time it rains, the streets turn into streams, and people have to drive or walk through floods. One year, the floods rose so high that millions of people—including Kotchakorn and her family—became homeless.

Kotchakorn believed there had to be a way to live with the floods. As she started researching, she discovered that her ancestors welcomed the excess water because they prepared for it. That's what she decided to do when Thailand's oldest university announced a design competition to celebrate its 100th birthday.

Now a landscape architect, she came up with a plan for a rooftop park built on a slight tilt. Rainwater would run down the slanted ground and be collected for the city to use. Tanks under the park could store one million gallons of rain so the parks would have plenty of water during the dry season. The rest would fall through plants and end up in a pond.

Her brilliant idea won the contest and became the blueprint for the first public park built in Thailand in 30 years! Kotchakorn called it "a big green crack at the heart of Bangkok," which is mostly concrete. She's working on making new "cracks" to allow even more of nature's beauty to push through.

BORN CIRCA 1981
THAILAND

"WE CAN TEACH PEOPLE HOW TO LIVE WITH WATER AGAIN, WHICH IS MUCH BETTER THAN FEARING IT." —KOTCHAKORN VORAAKHOM

ILLUSTRATION BY XUAN LOC XUAN

KRISTAL AMBROSE

ENVIRONMENTAL SCIENTIST

Once there was a girl named Kristal who was in love with the ocean. Kristal grew up in the Bahamas, which is a string of sandy-beached islands surrounded by shimmering turquoise waters. Every day, Kristal went for a swim with her dad, played on the shore with her siblings and cousins, and laughed at the waves lapping at her toes. She wanted to be a marine biologist so she could spend all her days by the sea.

But when Kristal was a teenager, she learned that the oceans were in danger. She got a job at an aquarium where she saw how plastic pollution was killing off animals and plants underwater. She once spent two days pulling plastic out of a sick sea turtle. Looking at the beautiful creature in the clinic, she vowed to never drop a piece of plastic again. Not only that, but she was also going to do everything she could to protect the oceans and all sea life.

In 2013, Kristal created the Bahamas Plastic Movement. She organized community beach cleanups and free environmental programs for kids. She even drafted a bill for the government to ban single-use plastics. How could she get the government to listen to her? she wondered. She had an idea. She invited her students to join her when she met with the environment and housing minister. Instead of calmly giving a speech, Kristal and her students brought tons of energy to the meeting. They banged on the tables and chanted, "We are the change. We are the solution. We can fix this plastic pollution!" There was no way the officials could forget them!

The Bahamian government was impressed, and in April 2018, they passed the bill! Kristal was thrilled. She knows there's still a lot to do to save the oceans. She also knows each of us can make a difference.

BORN DECEMBER 7, 1989
THE BAHAMAS

"YOUR VOICE MATTERS AND YOU DESERVE A SEAT AT THE TABLE IN MAKING DECISIONS THAT IMPACT YOUR FUTURE AND THE HEALTH OF THE PLANET."
—KRISTAL AMBROSE

ILLUSTRATION BY KETURAH ARIEL

LOKI SCHMIDT

CONSERVATIONIST

Loki loved flowers more than anything. Instead of reading storybooks, young Loki poured over the pictures in *Flora von Deutschland* (Flowers of Germany) until she knew the names of all the plants in her neighborhood. On the weekends, Loki visited the botanical garden with her family to discover new, exciting plants from around the world. She delighted in seeing delicate orchids and colorful new species of roses.

But one thing Loki understood about flowers very early was that they were fragile. The bouquets her father brought home to their family's tiny, gas-lit apartment always withered in two days.

As a grown-up, Loki became a teacher and shared her love of plants with her students. When Loki's husband was elected chancellor of West Germany, many doors opened for her and her mission to save wildflowers from habitat loss and other threats. She started an exchange program where gardeners in different countries could share plants. And she fought to build more botanical gardens to preserve endangered species and teach people about conservation.

She traveled the world, observing and documenting rare plant life from Kenya to the Galapagos Islands. On one trip, she discovered a new pineapple species in Mexico. It was named *Pitcairnia loki-schmidtii* in her honor!

Loki also started a Flower of the Year award! Each year, she showcased Germany's precious—and endangered—wildflowers. One year, she'd highlight the bright yellow petals of the mountain arnica. And the next, she'd celebrate the alpine snowbell with its little purple bell-shaped blooms.

As a child, Loki had wanted to be surrounded by all the flowers in her books. Through a life of advocacy, the entire world became her garden.

MARCH 3, 1919–OCTOBER 21, 2010
GERMANY

"I'VE BEEN TALKING ABOUT CONSERVATION FOR 100 YEARS, BUT WHO LISTENED TO A TEACHER FROM HAMBURG?"
—LOKI SCHMIDT

ILLUSTRATION BY VANESSA LOVEGROVE

LUCIE PINSON

CLIMATE ACTIVIST

O nce upon a time, a young woman named Lucie took on a terrible foe: coal pollution. But she couldn't just ball up her fists and fight the carbon dioxide in the hazy air. She had to be clever to win her war.

Lucie grew up in Nantes, a lively city on the Loire River in France. She traveled across the world to attend college in South Africa. There she saw the pollution created by coal plants up close. *Sure, coal is an energy source, and we all need energy*, she thought. *But, at what cost?* Burning coal pollutes the air and sends carbon dioxide into the atmosphere, where it wraps around the Earth like a giant blanket. It traps heat, warms the planet, and fuels climate change. It also produces ash that ends up in lakes, ponds, and rivers.

Horrified, Lucie found out that new coal plants were popping up all over the world, mostly in developing countries. *Who is paying for all these coal mines and factories?* she wondered. She found her answer close to home. Three French banks had loaned billions and billions of dollars to the coal industry. How could she convince them to stop?

She joined with other environmentalists to protest new coal projects. They gathered and marched and cut up their bank cards! Lucie took her quest to the press. She wanted everyone to know what their banks were supporting. With numbers and bar graphs and heartbreaking stories of illness and destroyed land, she began changing minds. It took years of educating people and lobbying executives. And by 2017, every bank in France agreed with Lucie. They would no longer pay for new coal projects.

Lucie has won many battles. But her fight is not over.

BORN NOVEMBER 4, 1985
FRANCE

ILLUSTRATION BY
SARAH LOULENDO

"I DISCOVERED WHAT
THE MOST POLLUTING
INDUSTRY IN THE WORLD
IS: FINANCE. AND I
DECIDED TO TAKE IT ON."
—LUCIE PINSON

LUCY KING

ZOOLOGIST

As a kid, Lucy loved running free with the animals that roamed the farms where she grew up in Lesotho and Kenya.

While her dog chased away snakes, Lucy raced through dirt paths on her bike or rode on a fast little pony. She loved digging below the surface of the river near her house. Most days, she came home covered in mud.

On special occasions, her parents would take the family camping at wildlife parks in South Africa. At night, she could hear massive elephants gently stomping outside their tent! But during the day, big electric fences prevented communities from getting close to the beautiful beasts.

Lucy understood the park's owners wanted to keep people safe, but to her, the fences were a mistake. They kept people afraid of the animals, and they imprisoned the seven-ton pachyderms. *There has to be another way to protect people and respect animals at the same time*, she thought. Later, Lucy and her professor stumbled on a simple yet brilliant solution.

In the communities they were studying, farmers and elephants were at war. The hungry elephants would gobble up the farmers' crops. Or they'd trample the plants to get to the food and water in people's homes.

When Lucy and her professor learned from local herders that elephants avoid beehives, Lucy devised a plan. She'd make a beehive fence! As soon as the elephants heard the buzz of the bees, they'd run. The farmers' crops and water tanks stayed safe—and so did the elephants! Even sweeter, the farmers got to sell the delicious honey and keep some for themselves.

But sweetest of all for Lucy was finding a natural way for animals and people to safely live side by side—just as she did as a mud-caked kid.

BORN OCTOBER 30, 1977
UNITED KINGDOM AND KENYA

ILLUSTRATION BY
JENNIFER M POTTER

"I DO SEE MORE
WOMEN COMING
TO THE FOREFRONT
NOW TO THINK
DIFFERENTLY AND
MORE BOLDLY ABOUT
THE CHALLENGES
WE FACE."
—LUCY KING

MARGARET ATWOOD

AUTHOR

Once upon a time, there was a girl named Margaret who wrote poetic essays about her pet praying mantis. She was fascinated by how smart the little critter was. She even trained it to walk up her arm and drink out of a spoon!

Margaret also had a pet butterfly. For her, tiny creeping, buzzing, or flying creatures were just as vibrant a part of life as the fungi and the woodlands she loved to observe. Her father was a biologist who studied forest insects. And his work took the family through some of the wildest woods in Canada.

As she grew up, her interest in the wonders of the natural world and the role science could play in it inspired her more and more. In school, she wrote an operetta featuring a teddy bear made of wool who was sad that he shrunk every time he was washed. When he fell in love with a princess made of scientifically created fabric, he got his happy ending—a baby made of a wool blend that did not shrink in the dryer.

Margaret expanded on these themes when she became a published author. One of her most celebrated works is a three-book series about a future society suffering from a distorted relationship between nature and science. Her words got readers all over the world thinking more seriously about climate change. Margaret encourages people to consider the role they can play to protect the planet and then to take action. She wants the next generation to enjoy the enchanted harmony she experienced as a child with her pet insects and the wild mushrooms and thickets of trees in the wilderness.

BORN NOVEMBER 18, 1939

CANADA

40

"THERE ARE INFINITELY POSSIBLE FUTURES, AND WHICH ONE WE GET WILL DEPEND ON THE DECISIONS WE MAKE NOW."
—MARGARET ATWOOD

ILLUSTRATION BY
KASIA BOGDAŃSKA

MARJORY STONEMAN DOUGLAS

JOURNALIST AND CONSERVATIONIST

SCAN TO HEAR MORE!

Once there was a girl named Marjory who visited a hot, swampy land called Florida when she was just four years old. In Florida, there were alligators as big as bicycles, swarms of hungry mosquitoes, and humidity that made the air thick and soupy. Marjory loved the place anyway. "I never forgot the quality of the tropic light," she wrote years later.

Marjory returned to Florida to live when she was 25 years old. She took a job at the *Miami Herald* and began writing about civil rights and women's suffrage. She called out terrible injustice in neighborhoods where Black people didn't have electricity or basic plumbing.

Miami was a bustling city. And just next door, there were thousands of square miles of buggy swampland known as the Everglades. Politicians wanted to drain the area and build houses on the land. But when Marjory visited the Everglades, she didn't see a problem that needed to be fixed. Instead, she saw egrets of many colors, lazy manatees, and little green lizards darting up tree trunks. She saw breezy marshes, flooded savannahs, and tall, slim sawgrass growing out of the water.

The Everglades is home to nine distinct ecosystems. Marjory knew that if they were destroyed, Florida would lose a vital water supply. It would also lose the great herons that swooped overhead and the sleek panthers that stalked through the mangroves—and thousands of other species of wildlife.

She published a best-selling book that combined science, history, and her personal experiences to spread the word about the magic of this "river of grass." Marjory continued working to protect the Everglades throughout her long life. She died in Florida at age 108.

APRIL 7, 1890–MAY 14, 1998

UNITED STATES OF AMERICA

ILLUSTRATION BY
NICOLE RIFKIN

"THERE ARE NO OTHER
EVERGLADES IN THE WORLD."
—MARJORY STONEMAN DOUGLAS

MYA-ROSE CRAIG

ORNITHOLOGIST AND ACTIVIST

Once there was a girl who loved birds. Nimble finches, patient owls, gangly herons—each bird taught Mya-Rose something different about itself and the world they shared. She wanted to see all the birds—all 10,000 species that hopped, flew, perched, and soared. She spent countless hours outdoors with her family and other birders in the English countryside, blogging about her adventures as Birdgirl.

But when Mya-Rose was 13, she realized she had spent so much time looking through her binoculars that she hadn't noticed something very significant about her fellow birders. While Mya-Rose and her mother were Bangladeshi, everyone else in her birding community was white. This didn't sit well with Mya-Rose. *Didn't nature belong to everyone?*

Mya-Rose's first mission had been to see as many birds as she could. And she had, seeing half the world's birds by the time she was 11 years old. She marveled at the tiny, busy wings of a hummingbird and the bright blue neck of the southern cassowary (which is more like a dinosaur than a modern bird!).

Her new mission would be to share birding—and all of nature—with as many kids as possible. Mya-Rose would create a flock of young birders of color committed to protecting the Earth for generations to come.

Mya-Rose started a camp and used social media to recruit Black and brown teenagers. She had read a statistic that really bothered her: less than 1 percent of environmental professionals were people of color. Well, that wouldn't be the case for long if Mya-Rose had anything to say about it. Today, her camp has helped hundreds of young people of color discover the joy of being present in nature.

BORN MAY 7, 2002

UNITED KINGDOM

"THE COUNTRYSIDE AND
WILD ENVIRONMENT HAVE
DIFFERENT VOICES AND
DIFFERENT PEOPLE."
—MYA-ROSE CRAIG

ILLUSTRATION BY
JULIA KUO

NEMONTE NENQUIMO

CLIMATE ACTIVIST

SCAN TO HEAR MORE!

Once upon a time there was a girl named Nemonte who lived in the Amazon jungle in Ecuador. She loved everything about her home—the cool dirt floors of her hut, the playful songs of the toucans in the trees, the achiote fruit that she crushed and used as face paint. She especially loved to hear her elders talk about how her Indigenous community, the Waorani, had protected this land for thousands of years.

But one day, when Nemonte was 12, she visited one of her aunts who lived near an oil well. She was shocked by the loud drilling and the flames and smoke shooting out of the well. She heard stories about the water turning black from oil spills, poisoning people and animals. Oil companies were knocking down trees, drilling under the rain forest, and making it impossible for Indigenous people and animals to live there.

Nemonte was terrified—and energized. "With a lot of courage, strength, and anger, I started to fight," she said. Nemonte talked to her village leaders and organized assemblies. She helped map out the Waorani territories, circulated petitions, installed solar panels, and collected rainwater.

Still, in 2018, Ecuador's government offered to sell seven million acres of Amazon forest to oil companies. Nemonte had had enough. She knew the Waorani people had a right to those lands, so she sued the government.

When the judge tried to rush through the case, Nemonte and a group of women sang so loud they shut down the court!

In April 2019, the verdict came back in favor of Nemonte and the Waorani. She helped safeguard 500,000 acres of Amazonian rain forest. And she made it clear that the planet is sacred, and it will take all of us to save it.

BORN 1986
ECUADOR

"THE JUNGLE AND THE GREEN AMAZON GIVE US LIFE AND GIVE LIFE TO THE PLANET."

—NEMONTE NENQUIMO

ILLUSTRATION BY
SOFÍA ACOSTA-VAREA
(LA SUERTE)

PURNIMA DEVI BARMAN

WILDLIFE BIOLOGIST

When Purnima's neighbors looked up into a tree and saw a giant feathered creature with an enormous beak and an orange pouch on its neck, they saw a bad omen—a dirty pest that brought bad luck. But Purnima saw something different. She saw a beautiful bird that helped the planet. It was a greater adjutant stork, known in the Assam region of India as the *hargila*, or bone-swallower.

The hargila is a scavenger. It will eat just about anything, including dead, rotting animals. Some people think scavengers are gross even though they are an important part of every ecosystem. When they eat, they clean up the environment. They crunch up bones, digest them, and return nutrients to the earth. But their nests and their droppings smell awful.

Purnima was working on her PhD in ecology and wildlife biology when she got a call that changed her life. *Help!* A man was cutting down trees with hargila nests in them. Baby birds were falling to the ground! Purnima rushed to try to reason with him. He yelled at her and shooed her away. *How can I make everyone understand how important these birds are?* she wondered.

She created a slideshow and added lyrics about the hargila to beloved folk songs. She gave women yarn so they could weave scarves and tablecloths with playful patterns featuring the hargila. And, in 2015, she decided to build the strongest army she could think of—an army of women. By 2019, more than 400 members of the Hargila Army were spreading Purnima's message.

The villagers, who once destroyed trees and hargila nests and mocked Purnima for loving the smelly creatures, are now proud of their local bird. Purnima brought a community together to save an endangered species.

BIRTHDATE UNKNOWN
INDIA

ILLUSTRATION BY
JUI TALUKDER

"HARGILA BIRDS HAVE BEAUTIFUL SKY BLUE
EYES, WHICH NEVER FAILS TO REMIND ME
THAT THE SKY IS THE LIMIT AND MOTIVATES
ME TO GIVE MY BEST IN MY WORK."
PURNIMA DEVI BARMAN

RACHEL CARSON

MARINE BIOLOGIST AND AUTHOR

Once there was a tiny bird singing its evening song, a spruce tree rustling in the wind, a bluefish leaping out of the surf, and a girl named Rachel who was amazed by it all.

Rachel grew up in a small house along the Allegheny River in Pennsylvania, where she loved exploring the forests and streams nearby and writing stories about everything she discovered.

After graduate school, Rachel got a job writing about marine biology for the US government. But there was so much more she needed to say. She wanted to explore the mysteries of nature. At night, when everyone in her home was asleep, Rachel stayed up writing. She imagined herself as a seagull or an eel, describing the watery world around her.

In 1941, Rachel published her first book, *Under the Sea-Wind*. Readers were amazed by how she brought the ocean to life on the page. She bought a cottage by the sea and kept writing. She wanted readers to see that humans were just one tiny part of a huge extraordinary planet.

When people started using chemicals called pesticides on their crops to repel insects, Rachel saw a tragedy. The pesticides were poisoning animals, birds, and even humans. So she wrote a book called *Silent Spring*. In it, she described a world where there were no birds singing and no trees rustling. The world was silent because the chemicals had killed off all of these creatures.

Many companies making pesticides tried to stop Rachel from talking about her discoveries. But Rachel only got louder. She went before Congress to demand that the government protect the environment. She used her words to inspire millions and to celebrate all species on Earth.

MAY 27, 1907–APRIL 14, 1964
UNITED STATES OF AMERICA

ILLUSTRATION BY
SARAH WILKINS

"THOSE WHO CONTEMPLATE THE
BEAUTY OF THE EARTH FIND RESERVES
OF STRENGTH THAT WILL ENDURE AS
LONG AS LIFE LASTS."
RACHEL CARSON

WANGARI MAATHAI

CLIMATE ACTIVIST

SCAN TO HEAR MORE!

Born in a small village in central Kenya, Wangari grew up surrounded by spectacular trees. Some of them gave her family fruit or shade. Some protected the freshwater streams. Some were even thought to bring peace to anyone who stood nearby.

But all of them were endangered.

More and more forests were being cut down to make room for farms and produce charcoal for fuel.

Wangari went to school, which was rare for girls at that time in Kenya. She was an excellent student, especially in science, and she became the first female professor in East and Central Africa. But the biggest lesson Wangari learned was from the women in her village. They told her how hard it was to find firewood or fresh water now that the trees were being cut down. They told terrible tales of the streams drying up and the desert eroding the soil.

Wangari thought about how she could help the women and save the land. She wasn't afraid to start small and let her big idea grow. She and her friends planted some seedlings in old tin cans. They watered and nurtured the young plants until they were big enough to put in the ground. In time, there were rows of new trees reaching into the sky! The women collected more seeds and kept planting.

Since Wangari started the Green Belt Movement in 1977, more than 51 million trees have been planted! Wangari's movement not only helps the Earth, but it also empowers women and girls with meaningful work. In 2004, Wangari was awarded the Nobel Peace Prize. Of course, the first thing she did to celebrate was dig a hole in the warm soil and plant another tree.

APRIL 1, 1940–SEPTEMBER 25, 2011

KENYA

ILLUSTRATION BY
THANDIWE TSHABALALA

"WHEN WE PLANT TREES,
WE PLANT THE SEEDS OF
PEACE AND HOPE."
—WANGARI MAATHAI

WINONA LADUKE

ACTIVIST AND FARMER

Winona loved to argue. As a member of her high school debate team, she tackled challenging topics, like global politics and environmental issues.

She looked around the world and saw people—and big companies—who had terrible ideas about how to use the Earth and its resources. Winona often thought of each of these terrible ideas as a wiindigo—a giant monster from Ojibwe lore. According to legend, the Ojibwe people had fought the wiindigo hundreds of years ago and defeated it.

But the wiindigo was back in a new form. It was made up of nuclear power plants and mining projects and oil pipelines that poisoned the clean water in Winona's ancestral land. Winona had been taught that caring for the land was the single most important thing. Yet the new wiindigo harmed the land.

Winona knew that her people had to stop this monster. She became a grassroots organizer and activist, working on the front lines to protect the land from big companies with greedy schemes. She used her training as an economist to teach others about the possibility of building a new, better economy. Instead of burning up fossil fuels to ship goods thousands of miles across the globe, people could rely on local foods and products. Winona became a farmer, growing traditional Ojibwe wild rice and raising horses. She even ran for vice president of the United States—twice!

Throughout all of her battles with this modern-day wiindigo, Winona has used her voice—and her incredible powers of persuasion—to educate people and encourage them to live in harmony with the land.

BORN AUGUST 18, 1959
UNITED STATES OF AMERICA

"POWER IS IN THE EARTH. IT IS IN YOUR RELATIONSHIP TO THE EARTH."
—WINONA LADUKE

ILLUSTRATION BY DÉBORA ISLAS

WRITE YOUR STORY

DRAW YOUR PORTRAIT

CELEBRATE NATURE

These activities, designed by SeaLegacy and the Only One Collective, are just a few of the ways you can observe, learn about, celebrate, and advocate for nature and wildlife.

✦ SAY IT WITH PICTURES!

Go outside with a camera or some drawing supplies and try to capture the beauty of animals or nature in photos or drawings.

✦ SAY IT WITH WORDS!

Take a journal with you on a nature walk. Engage your senses. Take time to observe the sights, sounds, and smells you encounter. Write down what you see. Write a story that takes place in the area you observe. Use your descriptive powers to make the scenery vibrant in your story.

✦ WAVE YOUR MAGIC WAND

Imagine you have a magic wand. How would you use it to create a healthier planet? Draw a picture or write a story showing or describing what the natural world around you would look like after you wave your magic wand. Have you been to a place like that in real life?

✦ SPREAD THE WORD

Create a poster. Write a clear slogan or message about how a kid (or grown-up) can help in a conservation effort. Draw pictures that will grab people's attention or support your slogan. Then ask your teacher if you can hang it up in your classroom. Wouldn't it be great if your friends made posters too?!

✦ QUIZ YOUR FRIENDS!

Do you know what carbon is? Does your family? After doing some research, create a multiple choice quiz and test your friends and family.

✦ RESEARCH AND REPORT

Research endangered ocean animals. Choose one and write about its behavior and habitat. Explain why it is endangered and what people can do to protect it. Share your essay with your parents, family, or teachers. You could even turn it into a letter and send it to your local newspaper.

✦ MAKE SEA LIFE STICKERS!

1. Gather printer paper, scissors, packing tape, and parchment paper.
2. Draw or print an image of your favorite ocean animal on the printer paper. Cut out with scissors.
3. Place packing tape on the parchment paper, sticky side down. Make sure your image is smaller than the piece of tape.
4. Place the image on top of the packing tape. Put more packing tape over the image, sticky side down, until it's covered.
5. Cut around the image. Be sure to leave a border around it.
6. Peel off the parchment paper and display your ocean pal wherever you'd like!

A NOTE FROM SEALEGACY AND THE ONLY ONE COLLECTIVE

We often hear that our planet is in trouble, but what we don't hear enough is that we have the power to save it. At SeaLegacy and the Only One Collective, we work to save our planet by protecting our oceans, but we can't do it alone. We need Rebel Girls like you to take big steps this decade to help keep our planet thriving—and protecting the ocean is one of the best places to start. From tiny plankton to the mighty blue whale, the plants and animals that live in the sea help fight climate change. They store up to 10 times more carbon than plants and creatures on land. The ocean is a beautiful and powerful place that offers the solutions we need to save the world. Help us to keep it thriving!

To learn more about SeaLegacy and the Only One Collective, ask your parents to help you check out *www.sealegacy.org* and *www.only.one*.

LIVE GREEN

Research shows that the people most likely to be affected by climate change are women. They are also the best advocates to fight it. Combating climate change will require governments and businesses to make huge changes. But people making changes in their day-to-day lives can help too. Humanitarian Zainab Salbi, from Daughters for Earth, shared with Rebel Girls some tips and activities for environmentally friendly practices you can adopt today.

HAVE A PLANT-BASED SNACK

Reducing the amount of meat you eat helps lower your carbon footprint. That doesn't mean you need to become a vegetarian if you aren't one already. Start small by incorporating a plant-based snack into your day.

- Make a rainbow fruit salad. Chop up strawberries, orange, mango, kiwi, blueberries, and grapes. Place them in a row and voilà!
- Sprinkle a handful of granola over your favorite flavor of yogurt. For an extra pop of sweetness, add a dollop of honey.
- Make apple stackers! With a grown-up's help or permission, cut half an apple into thin slices. Spread your favorite nut butter on a few slices and top them with other slices for a fresh take on mini sandwiches.

CELEBRATE ALL THINGS REUSABLE

Make your reusable water bottle more fun by personalizing it.

1. Make a list of empowering words that make you feel confident, like *brave, strong, kind, resilient, powerful, passionate,* or *magical.*
2. Gather letter stickers or cut out letters from old magazines. Use them to add your chosen words to your bottle. If you're using letters from magazines, place them face-down on the sticky side of clear packaging tape, then tape them to your bottle.
3. Decorate your bottle with any other stickers or images that make you happy!
4. Always carry your water bottle with you!

GO OUTSIDE!

Spending time outside reduces the amount of time you spend using devices that require energy. Being in nature also helps you appreciate all the amazing forms of life around us. You could:

✦ Go for a hike with your family.
✦ Set up an outside obstacle course.
✦ Grab binoculars and go bird-watching!

TRANSFORM A T-SHIRT

Clothing often ends up in landfills, which adds to the climate crisis. When you can, make old clothes new again. Here's one way—Inspired by Daughters for Earth—to revive an old T-shirt.

1. Use fabric paint to make a blue circle in the center of your shirt. Let it dry.
2. Tape a piece of paper to the wall. Stand in front of it facing the side.
3. Have a grown-up shine a flashlight on you, while tracing your silhouette.
4. Cut out your profile and place it in the center of the blue circle. Trace around it with green fabric paint.
5. Fill in and decorate however you'd like!

COMMIT TO HELPFUL HABITS

Carry a reusable tote.

Choose nonplastic toys and games.

Buy locally made food and locally grown produce.

Give the gift of locally grown flowers.

Reduce food waste by eating leftovers.

Shop at thrift stores or buy from sustainable clothing brands.

Choose clothes made from natural fibers like cotton, wool, silk, or hemp.

Use paper products made from bamboo.

Plant a native tree, flower, or vegetable inside your home or in your community.

ABOUT DAUGHTERS FOR EARTH

Daughters for Earth is made up of mothers and grandmothers, daughters and partners, visionaries, baristas, pilots, surgeons, farmers, cleaners, teachers, servers, leaders, and more. They appeal to women everywhere to look inside themselves, roll up their sleeves, and take the lead in preserving land and combating climate change. They fund women who are preserving land, making it safe for wild animals to return, and farming it in a way that allows earth to regenerate itself. *www.daughtersforearth.org*

MORE STORIES!

For more stories about amazing women and girls, check out other Rebel Girls books.

LISTEN TO MORE EMPOWERING STORIES ON THE REBEL GIRLS APP!

Download the app to listen to beloved Rebel Girls stories, as well as brand-new tales of extraordinary women. Filled with the adventures and accomplishments of women from around the world and throughout history, the Rebel Girls app is designed to entertain, inspire, and build confidence in listeners everywhere.

THE ILLUSTRATORS

Twenty-five extraordinary female artists from all over the world illustrated the portraits in this book.

ABOUT REBEL GIRLS

REBEL GIRLS is a global, multi-platform empowerment brand dedicated to helping raise the most inspired and confident global generation of girls through content, experiences, products, and community. Originating from an international best-selling children's book, Rebel Girls amplifies stories of real-life women throughout history, geography, and field of excellence. With a growing community of nearly 20 million self-identified Rebel Girls spanning more than 100 countries, the brand engages with Generation Alpha through its book series, award-winning podcast, events, and merchandise. With the 2021 launch of the Rebel Girls app, the company has created a flagship destination for girls to explore a wondrous world filled with inspiring true stories of extraordinary women.

Join the Rebel Girls' community:

✦ Facebook: facebook.com/rebelgirls
✦ Instagram: @rebelgirls
✦ Twitter: @rebelgirlsbook
✦ Web: rebelgirls.com
✦ App: rebelgirls.com/app

If you liked this book, please take a moment to review it wherever you prefer!